THE HEALTH-WEALTH CONNECTION

How Wellness Science Drives Financial Success

CONSULTORIA IA

TO OUR FAMILY

CONTENTS

BRIEF OVERVIEW

The Health-Wealth Connection: How Wellness Science Drives Financial Success delves into the transformative relationship between personal wellness and financial prosperity. This book reveals how prioritizing health—both mental and physical—paves the way for smarter decisions, increased productivity, and sustainable wealth. Through chapters exploring the science of stress resilience, cognitive optimization, and the compounding effects of healthy habits, readers will learn actionable strategies to leverage their well-being for financial growth. Packed with practical advice and inspiring case studies, this guide empowers individuals to invest in themselves and achieve unparalleled success in life and business.

TARGET AUDIENCE

The target audience for The Health-Wealth Connection: How Wellness Science Drives Financial Success includes:

1. Entrepreneurs and Business Professionals: Individuals seeking to optimize their productivity, leadership, and decision-making abilities by incorporating wellness strategies.

2. Self-Help and Personal Development Enthusiasts: Readers interested in books that combine health, personal growth, and financial success.

3. Corporate Leaders and Managers: Professionals looking for ways to foster a healthier work environment that boosts team performance and profitability.

4. Financial Planners and Coaches: Advisors who wish to integrate holistic approaches when guiding clients toward achieving financial goals.

5. Health and Wellness Advocates: People passionate about the intersection of health and finance, eager to explore how lifestyle choices impact economic outcomes.

WHY READ THIS BOOK

The Health-Wealth Connection: How Wellness Science Drives Financial Success is a must-read for anyone looking to unlock their full potential by understanding the crucial link between health and financial success. Here's why you should read this book:

1. Science-Backed Insights: The book blends cutting-edge wellness science with financial wisdom, offering proven techniques to enhance both mind and body for optimal performance and profitability.

2. Actionable Strategies: It's not just theory—each chapter provides practical steps and routines that can be implemented immediately to improve health and boost income.

3. Holistic Approach: Unlike other guides that focus solely on financial tactics or health advice, this book reveals how merging the two can create sustainable, long-term success.

4. Inspiring Case Studies: Real-world stories showcase how individuals and leaders have applied these principles to overcome challenges and achieve financial freedom.

5. Comprehensive Guidance: From stress management and mental clarity to building resilient habits, readers gain tools to maintain balance while thriving financially.

Reading this book equips you with the knowledge and motivation to prioritize your well-being as a fundamental part of achieving lasting financial success.

PREFACE

In a world where hustle and ambition are celebrated, it's easy to overlook the most vital component of success: our health. We've been conditioned to believe that financial achievement requires sacrificing well-being, but what if this mindset is flawed? What if the key to true, sustainable wealth lies in embracing health as the foundation of success?

The Health-Wealth Connection: How Wellness Science Drives Financial Success was born out of a simple but powerful realization: the path to financial prosperity is most effective when it begins with wellness. Drawing on years of research, personal stories, and practical strategies, this book aims to shift your perspective and show that peak financial performance isn't just a result of hard work; it's a byproduct of a healthy mind and body.

Whether you are an entrepreneur scaling your business, a professional striving for peak productivity, or someone looking to create a more balanced, rewarding life, this book provides the roadmap. You'll discover the science behind how mental clarity, stress resilience, and daily wellness routines can translate into smarter decisions, more significant opportunities, and enhanced wealth.

I invite you to rethink success and take this journey where health isn't the price you pay, but the investment that makes financial achievement inevitable.

Welcome to a new era where wellness drives wealth.

CHAPTER 1: THE FOUNDATION OF WEALTH – WHY YOUR HEALTH IS YOUR GREATEST ASSET

When we talk about wealth, our minds often leap to images of expansive bank accounts, luxury cars, and sprawling real estate. Society teaches us that financial abundance is the benchmark of success, a reward for years of dedication and shrewd decision-making. Yet, one essential truth remains overlooked: health is the cornerstone upon which all wealth is built. Without it, the pursuit of financial prosperity is fragile, unsustainable, and ultimately hollow.

It's easy to dismiss health as just a part of the equation—something separate from financial planning and wealth accumulation. But this view ignores the profound interconnections between physical wellness, mental acuity, and financial outcomes. In reality, these elements are intertwined so intricately that neglecting one can unravel the others. In this chapter, we will uncover why investing in your health is one of the most strategic financial decisions you can make, explore the tangible and intangible benefits of wellness, and illustrate how health directly contributes to long-term prosperity.

The Vital Connection Between Energy and Productivity

Picture the most successful people you know or have read about. Whether it's CEOs of global corporations, influential entrepreneurs, or pioneers in any field, there is a common trait they share: an abundance of energy. This vitality is not coincidental—it is the result of intentional habits that prioritize health. The connection between energy and productivity is as straightforward as it is impactful. A body that is well-nourished, rested, and fit will naturally perform better, not just physically but cognitively.

Research has shown that regular exercise increases productivity by enhancing concentration and mental sharpness. Aerobic activities like running, swimming, and cycling increase blood flow to the brain, which facilitates better memory, creativity, and problem-solving skills. The capacity to tackle complex problems without fatigue or mental fog is essential in high-stakes environments, making it clear that physical health and peak professional performance are inseparable.

A survey published by the Harvard Business Review highlighted that employees who regularly engage in physical exercise report higher levels of happiness and work satisfaction. This is not a trivial statistic—it hints at the deeper relationship between health and professional performance. Companies have taken notice, investing millions in wellness programs designed to boost employee well-being, and by extension, their bottom lines. In fact, the return on investment (ROI) for corporate wellness initiatives has been shown to be as high as $3 for every $1 spent.

For individuals, the same principles apply. By investing time and resources into physical wellness—through regular exercise, balanced nutrition, and sufficient sleep—you're essentially giving yourself a competitive advantage in the workplace and in entrepreneurial ventures. The energy you gain from maintaining good health translates into increased productivity, higher earning potential, and more robust career advancement.

Health's Influence on Decision-Making and Risk Management

The financial world thrives on decisions: investments, career moves, strategic partnerships. These decisions can be transformative or catastrophic, and the ability to navigate them with clarity is paramount. Cognitive biases, fueled by stress or mental exhaustion, can lead to poor judgment. On the other hand, maintaining a baseline of good health can act as an antidote to these detrimental tendencies.

When your body is functioning at an optimal level, so is your brain. Research in neuroscience has demonstrated that exercise boosts the production of brain-derived neurotrophic factor (BDNF), a protein that promotes the growth and resilience of brain cells. This has direct implications for enhancing executive functions like strategic thinking, decision-making, and emotional regulation.

It is important to understand that decision-making is not a purely intellectual endeavor; it is also emotional. Chronic stress, fatigue, and poor nutrition exacerbate emotional responses, making people more likely to make impulsive or risk-averse decisions. For example, someone who is not taking care of their physical health may find themselves more prone to react to market volatility with panic selling or overly conservative investment strategies that limit growth potential. Conversely, individuals with robust health are better equipped to handle stress, consider long-term benefits, and execute decisions with greater confidence and clarity.

Financial success is inherently tied to the ability to manage and take risks wisely. When your mind is sharp and your body resilient, you are more likely to trust your judgment and act with boldness when opportunities arise. This is not to say that good health alone will make you a financial guru, but it certainly equips you with the mental and emotional tools necessary to excel in high-pressure financial environments.

The Compounding Costs of Neglect

Understanding the link between health and wealth isn't only about highlighting the positives; it also involves examining what happens when health is neglected. Chronic health issues such as diabetes, heart disease, and obesity don't just erode physical capabilities;

they come with significant financial consequences. Medical bills, medications, specialist consultations, and potential surgeries can accumulate rapidly, depleting savings and derailing financial plans.

According to the Centers for Disease Control and Prevention (CDC), chronic illnesses are among the most significant drains on personal and public finances. In the U.S., chronic diseases account for approximately 75% of all healthcare spending. For the individual, this means that poor health doesn't just lower quality of life—it actively undermines financial stability.

A particularly stark example of this is the cost of healthcare in retirement. Many people save diligently, only to discover that a substantial portion of their nest egg is consumed by unexpected medical expenses. The Fidelity Retiree Health Care Cost Estimate suggests that an average retired couple may need upwards of $300,000 for medical expenses during retirement. This figure doesn't include long-term care, which can add even more to the financial burden.

Neglecting health during one's younger years sets the stage for these costly consequences later. What's more, poor health can force early retirement, a reduced ability to work, or lower income potential. The ripple effects of not investing in health are as real as a market crash or a failed investment—both can leave you scrambling to recover financially.

Health as an Investment Strategy

With the evidence laid out, it's clear that investing in health is not a luxury; it's a necessity for financial security and prosperity. But what does this investment look like in practice? The answer lies in adopting a holistic approach to well-being that prioritizes physical, mental, and emotional health.

1. Prioritizing Sleep: It's easy to undervalue sleep in a culture that celebrates hustle and long work hours. However, the science is unequivocal: sleep deprivation impairs cognitive function, increases the likelihood of chronic diseases, and diminishes productivity. Treating sleep as a non-negotiable aspect of your daily routine is an investment that pays off through better decision-making and increased energy.

2. Balanced Nutrition: Nutrition is more than just calories and taste—it is fuel for the body and mind. A diet rich in whole foods like vegetables, fruits, lean proteins, and whole grains provides essential nutrients that enhance cognitive performance, mood stability, and immune function. Conversely, diets high in processed foods and sugar can lead to crashes in energy and focus, undermining productivity and overall well-being.

3. Regular Physical Activity: Exercise doesn't have to mean training for a marathon or spending hours at the gym. Even moderate daily activity, such as walking, yoga, or swimming, can yield substantial benefits. The key is consistency. Physical activity improves cardiovascular health, increases energy levels, and promotes the release of endorphins,

which are natural mood lifters. A healthier mood contributes to clearer thinking and more positive interactions—both vital in high-stakes business or professional settings.

4. Mindfulness and Stress Management: Chronic stress takes a toll on both mental and physical health, leading to fatigue, decreased cognitive ability, and a weakened immune system. Practices like mindfulness meditation, deep breathing, and other relaxation techniques have been proven to reduce stress levels and enhance focus. Making time for these practices can improve resilience and clarity when navigating difficult financial decisions.

Case Studies: Leaders Who Link Health and Wealth

History and modern success stories provide compelling examples of how health-first philosophies can contribute to wealth. Consider Richard Branson, founder of the Virgin Group. Known for his boundless energy, Branson attributes much of his business success to his commitment to fitness and wellness. He famously states that maintaining his physical health gives him an extra four hours of productivity every day. This additional time isn't just about being physically present; it's about being present and sharp enough to capitalize on opportunities that others may overlook due to exhaustion or distraction.

Another case is Arianna Huffington, founder of The Huffington Post and CEO of Thrive Global. After collapsing from exhaustion in 2007, she became an advocate for sleep and well-being as critical components of professional success. Her approach underscores that health is not just complementary to success but foundational to it.

These leaders didn't merely stumble upon the realization that health is pivotal; they learned it through experience. Their stories illustrate that wellness is not an afterthought or a hobby—it is a non-negotiable part of a sustainable strategy for success.

The Multiplier Effect of Health Investments

Investing in health pays dividends that extend beyond personal well-being. Healthy individuals contribute positively to their families, inspire colleagues, and create a culture of growth and resilience in their professional environments. This multiplier effect can create communities and workplaces where shared prosperity is built on shared wellness.

Consider how this manifests in family life. A parent who prioritizes health sets an example for children, teaching them the value of wellness from an early age. This modeling doesn't just promote better habits; it reduces the potential for future medical expenses, instills discipline, and fosters a mindset that views health as an asset.

On a larger scale, businesses that support health initiatives see lower absenteeism, higher employee engagement, and better overall performance. The link between a company's collective health and its success is a testament to the wider impact that investing in wellness can have.

The Real Wealth of Nations

The old adage "health is wealth" rings truer than ever in the context of modern financial success.

Health is not just an abstract concept but a tangible asset that influences every aspect of our ability to achieve and maintain financial prosperity. From the energy needed to fuel ambitious projects to the cognitive sharpness required for critical decision-making, health amplifies our capabilities and shields us from the risks of both life and the financial world.

As we move forward in this exploration of the health-wealth connection, remember that each action taken toward better health is an investment in a more secure, prosperous future. In the balance of life's pursuits, health remains the greatest asset, underpinning not only our financial ambitions but also the quality and longevity of the wealth we seek to build.

When we envision wealth, our thoughts often gravitate toward tangible assets: homes, investments, luxury goods. Financial freedom, we're taught, is the pinnacle of success. Yet there's a truth that underpins all monetary accomplishments—a truth so essential that its neglect can make the pursuit of riches feel futile: health is our most vital asset. Without it, even the most robust financial portfolio can become meaningless. This chapter delves into why prioritizing health is the most strategic step toward securing not just financial wealth but a balanced, fulfilling life.

The Unbreakable Link Between Health and Productivity

Consider the CEOs and high achievers who seem to tackle complex challenges effortlessly. What sets them apart is not just their business acumen but their boundless energy and mental clarity. Studies support the notion that health underpins productivity. For instance, research from the Journal of Occupational and Environmental Medicine shows that employees who prioritize regular physical activity are 15% more productive than their sedentary counterparts. This improvement translates into approximately 6.5 hours of extra productivity per week.

The reason is simple: physical activity stimulates the release of endorphins, enhances mood, and increases oxygen flow to the brain, which optimizes cognitive functions. This means sharper decision-making, better problem-solving, and sustained focus—all crucial for high-stakes environments. For those who lead companies, develop startups, or hold influential roles, these advantages can mean the difference between a well-timed strategic decision and a missed opportunity.

The Cost of Fatigue on Your Bottom Line

The modern lifestyle—long work hours, endless meetings, and constant digital connectivity—often leads to chronic fatigue. The economic implications of exhaustion are staggering. According to the RAND Corporation, fatigue-related productivity losses cost the U.S. economy $411 billion annually. Workers who sleep fewer than six hours per night are 2.9% less productive than their well-rested peers, equating to approximately 1.23 million lost working days each year.

Imagine the compounded effect of fatigue on an individual level. A tired mind is more prone to making impulsive decisions, overlooking details, and succumbing to stress. For example, a fatigued financial analyst might misinterpret data, leading to suboptimal investment choices. Over time, such lapses can undermine long-term financial growth and career trajectory.

Cognitive Sharpness: The Ultimate Tool for Financial Success

Decision-making and risk management form the backbone of any successful financial strategy. These capabilities are directly linked to cognitive health. A 2018 study published in Frontiers in Neuroscience found that regular aerobic exercise increases the size of the hippocampus—the part of the brain responsible for memory and learning. This neuroplasticity facilitates better analytical thinking, emotional regulation, and long-term planning.

The reverse is also true. Poor health can impair judgment and increase susceptibility to cognitive biases. For instance, chronic stress triggers the release of cortisol, which can cloud thinking and lead to short-term, fear-based decision-making. In a financial context, this might manifest as an investor panicking during market dips and selling assets at a loss instead of holding on for long-term gains. In contrast, those who maintain their health through regular exercise and stress management techniques are more equipped to stay composed, allowing them to navigate financial markets and career challenges with confidence and foresight.

The Expensive Reality of Neglecting Health

Neglecting health can have profound economic consequences that extend beyond lost productivity. Medical expenses from preventable chronic conditions can erode savings and cripple long-term financial plans. The Centers for Disease Control and Prevention (CDC) estimates that chronic diseases, such as heart disease, diabetes, and obesity, account for 75% of the $3.8 trillion in annual U.S. healthcare costs.

For individuals, the financial burden is staggering. The American Heart Association reports that cardiovascular disease alone costs the U.S. economy approximately $363 billion annually, encompassing healthcare services, medications, and lost productivity. For the average person, hospital stays and specialized treatments can rapidly drain even substantial savings.

Consider the financial implications of a diagnosis like Type 2 diabetes. According to the American Diabetes Association, the average cost of managing diabetes is about $16,750 per year, including medications, doctor visits, and lifestyle adjustments. Over two decades, this could amount to more than $335,000. This figure doesn't account for potential lost income due to reduced work capacity or early retirement. Now, compare that to the far more modest cost of preventive measures such as a gym membership, healthy food, and regular check-ups. The financial equation is clear: prevention is not just better than cure; it's more affordable.

Investing in Health: A Strategic Financial Move

Understanding that health is an investment is crucial for anyone serious about long-term financial growth. While this might sound abstract, it can be broken down into practical strategies that yield both immediate and compounding benefits.

1. Prioritizing Quality Sleep: The relationship between sleep and cognitive performance cannot be overstated. According to the National Sleep Foundation, adults who sleep 7-8 hours per night report significantly better focus and memory retention. Additionally, research from Harvard Medical School shows that poor sleep can increase the risk of financial errors by 20%, emphasizing that sufficient rest is as critical to financial stability as budgeting and saving.

2. Maintaining a Balanced Diet: The impact of nutrition on cognitive and physical health is well-documented. A study from The Lancet highlighted that diets high in processed foods and sugar can impair brain function and exacerbate fatigue, affecting productivity and mental health. On the other hand, diets rich in omega-3 fatty acids, vegetables, and lean proteins support optimal brain health, improving concentration and stress resilience.

3. Incorporating Regular Exercise: As highlighted by the American Journal of Psychiatry, regular physical activity can reduce the risk of depression by up to 26%. This is essential, as depression and anxiety can significantly hinder career performance and earning potential. Furthermore, exercise is linked to better cardiovascular health, which in turn lowers the likelihood of costly medical bills and ensures a longer, more productive career.

4. Adopting Stress Management Techniques: Chronic stress has financial implications that are often underestimated. According to The American Institute of Stress, workplace stress costs the U.S. over $300 billion annually in lost productivity and healthcare expenses. Simple, consistent practices like mindfulness meditation or deep-breathing exercises have been proven to reduce stress levels and enhance mental clarity. For instance, a study published in JAMA Internal Medicine revealed that individuals who practiced mindfulness for 30 minutes a day experienced a 20% reduction in stress markers.

Case Studies: Lessons from High Achievers

The stories of successful entrepreneurs and business leaders demonstrate that health isn't just an individual advantage—it's a business imperative. Take Jeff Bezos, for example. Known for being one of the most strategic thinkers of our time, Bezos famously prioritizes sleep, reportedly ensuring he gets eight hours each night. His rationale is straightforward: adequate rest enhances his ability to make high-quality decisions, a non-negotiable aspect of running Amazon.

Another illustrative example is Richard Branson, founder of the Virgin Group, who credits daily exercise as the key to his sustained energy and sharpness. He claims that a commitment to fitness gives him an edge that translates into about four extra hours of productive work each day. This isn't just a boast; it's a testament to the fact that the return on investment from health is measurable and substantial.

Long-Term Gains: Health's Role in Financial Independence

While immediate productivity and cognitive benefits are compelling, the long-term financial gains of prioritizing health are just as critical. One of the most striking examples of how poor health affects financial independence is the escalating cost of healthcare in retirement. Fidelity Investments projects that a 65-year-old couple retiring in 2023 will need approximately $315,000 for medical expenses throughout retirement, excluding long-term care. This underscores the importance of maintaining health during one's working years as an investment in future financial security.

Healthy individuals often find that they can work longer, should they choose to, without the physical and mental limitations that lead many into early retirement. This additional time in the workforce, especially in high-paying roles or entrepreneurial ventures, contributes significantly to building a more substantial financial cushion.

Tips for a Health-First Financial Strategy

To integrate health as a key component of your financial strategy, consider the following:

- View health expenses as investments, not costs: Allocate funds for high-quality food, gym memberships, and preventive healthcare. These "expenses" are investments in energy, productivity, and future medical savings.

- Schedule health as you would a meeting: Treat exercise, meal prep, and downtime as non-negotiable parts of your calendar. This structured approach ensures consistency and reaps long-term rewards.

- Leverage technology: Use fitness apps, sleep trackers, and mindfulness tools to keep your health on track. Studies from Behavioral Medicine show that individuals who track their fitness are 30% more likely to meet their health goals.

- Join a community: Whether it's a running club or a cooking class focused on healthy meals, a supportive community can increase accountability and motivation, further embedding wellness as a lifestyle.

Choosing to Prioritize Health Today

The numbers don't lie: health and wealth are more interconnected than we often acknowledge. Ignoring health in favor of career success might yield short-term gains but comes at the expense of long-term prosperity. On the other hand, integrating health into your financial strategy ensures you are equipped to capitalize on opportunities, maintain resilience in the face of challenges, and enjoy the fruits of your labor well into the future.

Health is not just a tool for wealth; it is the foundation upon which sustainable financial success is built. By prioritizing wellness today, you're not just enhancing your current productivity or sharpening your decision-making skills—you're securing a future where wealth is enjoyed in good health, free from the burdens of preventable medical issues. In this interconnected world of health and wealth, investing in your body and mind is the most strategic move you can make.

CHAPTER 2: BRAIN BOOSTS FOR BUSINESS – THE SCIENCE OF MENTAL CLARITY AND PROFITABILITY

T he Mental Edge in Business

In today's hypercompetitive business environment, mental clarity and focus aren't just assets—they're necessities. Leaders who master their minds have a significant edge, using heightened awareness and strategic thinking to outmaneuver competitors. Studies show that clarity, focus, and stress resilience can improve decision-making and increase productivity, ultimately driving profitability. For instance, a study from the American Psychological Association found that companies with low-stress work environments reported 37% higher employee productivity, translating directly to better financial outcomes.

The Science of Mental Clarity: A Business Advantage

1. Mental Sharpness for Decision-Making

Business leaders often face high-stakes decisions where every second counts. When the brain operates at its peak, decisions are faster, more accurate, and less influenced by cognitive biases. Neuroscience reveals that high mental clarity enhances activity in the prefrontal cortex, the area responsible for executive functions like planning, strategic thinking, and impulse control—qualities essential in business.

> Statistic: Research from Harvard University suggests that executives who regularly practice mental clarity exercises—like meditation or cognitive training—report a 20-30% boost in decision-making speed and accuracy. This increase in efficiency can lead to reduced operational costs, improved project outcomes, and faster time-to-market.

2. Focus: The Billion-Dollar Skill

Deep focus is one of the most valuable skills a business leader can cultivate. It's known that every interruption can take up to 23 minutes for the brain to refocus on the original task, a costly delay in fast-paced business environments. Tech giants like Google and Apple invest in focus-enhancing workshops for employees, recognizing that the collective ability to concentrate could be worth millions.

> Statistic: The McKinsey Global Institute found that high-performance individuals who can sustain focus in work tasks generate up to five times as much value as their counterparts, highlighting the direct link between mental focus and revenue generation.

Boosting Brain Health for Profitability

1. The Role of Physical Exercise in Cognitive Function

Physical health and mental acuity are deeply intertwined. Regular physical exercise has been shown to increase blood flow to the brain, fostering neuron growth and boosting mental agility. A study from the University of British Columbia found that regular aerobic exercise enhances the hippocampus—the part of the brain linked to memory and learning—by up to 2%, a small but significant improvement for memory retention and mental sharpness in demanding roles.

> Example: CEOs such as Mark Zuckerberg and Richard Branson make exercise a part of their daily routines, crediting it for their mental clarity and energy. Implementing regular physical activity into your lifestyle, even in short bursts, can not only enhance your health but sharpen your mind, directly affecting your capacity to innovate and lead.

2. Nutritional Power: Feeding the Brain

Just like any high-performance machine, the brain needs the right fuel to perform optimally. Studies indicate that diets rich in omega-3 fatty acids, antioxidants, and vitamins directly improve cognitive function. For example, omega-3 fatty acids, found in fish and flaxseed, are known to support cell membrane flexibility in brain neurons, promoting faster information processing.

> Statistic: A study published in "Neurology" found that adults with diets rich in omega-3s scored 26% higher on cognitive function tests compared to those with lower intakes. For business professionals, adopting a diet that supports brain health can sharpen memory, enhance problem-solving abilities, and improve overall cognitive performance.

Stress Management: The Foundation of Mental Resilience

1. The Cost of Unmanaged Stress

Chronic stress can lead to burnout, a state of mental and physical exhaustion that plagues many high-achievers. The World Health Organization (WHO) estimates that depression and anxiety disorders cost the global economy $1 trillion annually in lost productivity. Chronic stress is not only harmful to health but also detrimental to creativity and effective decision-making.

> Statistic: The American Institute of Stress reports that 80% of workers feel stressed on the job, with nearly half saying they need help in learning how to manage stress. As a

leader, managing stress isn't just about personal well-being; it's a critical step toward maintaining a productive and profitable work environment.

2. The Role of Meditation and Mindfulness

Meditation has become a mainstream solution for executives looking to boost their mental clarity and resilience. Studies from the National Center for Complementary and Integrative Health show that regular meditation can reduce stress, increase focus, and improve emotional regulation. Google's "Search Inside Yourself" program, a mindfulness-based emotional intelligence course, has demonstrated measurable increases in employee focus and satisfaction, impacting the company's bottom line.

> Example: Ray Dalio, founder of Bridgewater Associates, attributes much of his business success to daily meditation, citing the practice as essential for maintaining a clear mind and balanced emotions amidst the pressures of high-stakes investing.

Sleep as the Ultimate Performance Enhancer

1. The Productivity-Killing Effects of Sleep Deprivation

It's tempting to sacrifice sleep for more work hours, but science shows this is counterproductive. Inadequate sleep has been linked to memory problems, reduced creativity, and impaired judgment. According to a study published in "Nature," individuals who slept fewer than six hours per night for two weeks scored lower on cognitive tests than those who were legally intoxicated.

> Statistic: The RAND Corporation estimates that sleep deprivation costs the U.S. economy up to $411 billion annually. Leaders who prioritize quality sleep are more likely to enjoy sustained cognitive performance, sharper decision-making, and reduced risk of burnout.

2. How Sleep Enhances Creativity and Problem-Solving

Sleep plays a critical role in memory consolidation and problem-solving. REM sleep, the stage associated with dreaming, has been shown to aid in the creative problem-solving process, as the brain connects unrelated concepts and ideas. Many high-profile entrepreneurs and inventors report receiving creative breakthroughs during or after sleep, illustrating the critical role of rest in innovation and profitability.

> Example: Jeff Bezos, founder of Amazon, makes it a priority to get eight hours of sleep each night, believing that his quality of sleep contributes to clearer thinking and better business decisions.

Building a Brain-Healthy Company Culture

1. Promoting Mental Health Initiatives

Companies that actively promote mental health create a more resilient workforce, capable of adapting to challenges and driving innovation. A study by Deloitte found that organizations with mental health programs experience a 4:1 return on investment, as healthier, happier employees are more productive, loyal, and engaged.

> Example: Johnson & Johnson implemented a mental health program that reduced depression symptoms among employees by 33%, significantly lowering absenteeism and improving team morale. By investing in mental health resources, businesses create a culture that values well-being, ultimately leading to greater profitability.

2. Encouraging Breaks and Downtime for Mental Rejuvenation

Encouraging short, regular breaks throughout the workday can significantly improve productivity. Breaks allow the brain to reset, making room for creativity and problem-solving upon returning to tasks. The Pomodoro Technique, which involves 25 minutes of focused work followed by a 5-minute break, is an example of a time-tested method for improving productivity and reducing burnout.

> Statistic: Research from the Draugiem Group showed that employees who took regular breaks were 11% more productive than their peers who worked without stopping. Leaders who adopt and encourage similar strategies can foster a healthier, more efficient work environment.

Leveraging Mental Wellness for Long-Term Success

Integrating brain-boosting practices into your daily routine and fostering a brain-healthy company culture is more than just a wellness trend; it's a proven path to financial success. From enhanced focus and creativity to reduced stress and better decision-making, mental clarity translates into a powerful advantage for leaders. As science continues to reveal the undeniable link between mental wellness and business profitability, investing in brain health becomes not just a personal commitment but a strategic business move.

By making these evidence-based lifestyle changes, you can unlock a level of clarity, focus, and resilience that drives both personal fulfillment and business success, laying the groundwork for a thriving, sustainable career.

How Sharp is Your Business Edge?

Are your business decisions as sharp as they could be? Are you operating at peak mental clarity? What if your mental well-being could be the difference between profit and loss?

In today's fast-paced, high-stakes business landscape, mental clarity isn't a luxury—it's a necessity. Leaders and entrepreneurs are constantly facing a stream of complex decisions, making strategic vision and quick, accurate thinking more critical than ever. And science shows that mental well-being plays a crucial role in fostering these skills. Studies reveal that enhanced clarity, focus, and stress resilience improve productivity, boost decision-making, and drive profitability. For example, companies with low-stress environments report 37% higher productivity levels—a significant competitive edge in any industry.

Yet, as mental wellness gains recognition in the business world, leaders face new and complex challenges. We are beginning to understand that the future of successful leadership hinges on a blend of personal mental resilience and fostering a workplace culture that values well-being. This chapter explores the science of brain health, how it directly impacts business outcomes, and the critical challenges ahead for leaders who aim to thrive in an increasingly demanding environment.

The Science of Mental Clarity: A Business Edge Worth Investing In

1. Mental Sharpness for Complex Decision-Making

Business success today depends heavily on rapid, high-quality decisions. Leaders must be able to sift through complex information, make confident choices, and pivot quickly when necessary. Neuroscience has shown that mental clarity improves the brain's executive functions—specifically the prefrontal cortex, which handles planning, strategic thinking, and impulse control. These skills are indispensable when managing high-stakes decisions in competitive markets.

> Statistic: According to Harvard researchers, executives who practice regular mental clarity exercises, like meditation or cognitive training, report a 20-30% boost in decision-making speed and accuracy. For organizations, this translates to better project outcomes, improved operational efficiency, and faster product launches.

2. Focus: The Multi-Million Dollar Skill

Deep, undistracted focus is one of the rarest and most valuable assets in modern business. Interruptions in work can take up to 23 minutes to recover from, meaning that even brief distractions lead to costly productivity losses. With major corporations like Google investing in focus-enhancement workshops, it's clear that they see the return on investment in helping employees maintain concentration.

> Statistic: McKinsey Global Institute's research shows that high-performing individuals capable of deep focus can generate up to five times more value for their organizations compared to others. This powerful link between focused work and financial performance underscores why mental clarity is a true asset in driving revenue growth.

Brain Health and Future Profitability: Three Major Challenges

As we look to the future, the relationship between brain health and profitability will only grow stronger, but leaders face three distinct challenges in integrating mental wellness practices into their lives and their organizations:

1. The Escalating Mental Demands of a Hyperconnected World

As technology advances, leaders are expected to process massive amounts of data and make real-time decisions, often with limited downtime. This hyperconnectivity can be mentally taxing, leading to fatigue and reduced cognitive performance. Yet, high expectations persist, and burnout is increasingly common In response, companies and leaders must adopt a proactive approach, not only to prevent burnout but to cultivate sustainable mental performance practices.

> Example: Many executives are turning to digital detoxes and scheduled "deep work" blocks to protect their mental bandwidth. Companies that support these practices are finding that giving employees focused, uninterrupted time enhances their work quality and decision-making skills, ultimately boosting the company's bottom line.

2. Balancing Brain Health with Non-Stop Productivity Culture

The drive for constant productivity can undermine mental wellness, creating a cycle of stress that affects both leaders and their teams. Although research clearly shows that mental clarity leads to better performance, many business cultures still glorify overwork. Shifting these deeply ingrained cultural norms toward valuing well-being over constant productivity will be a substantial but necessary challenge.

> Statistic: The World Health Organization reports that stress-related illnesses cost businesses approximately $1 trillion globally in lost productivity each year. Businesses that prioritize mental health, by offering mindfulness programs and mental health days, see higher productivity rates and reduced absenteeism—factors that directly contribute to profitability.

3. Adapting to the Demands of a Remote and Hybrid Workforce

The rise of remote and hybrid work presents unique mental health challenges. Many professionals report that remote work blurs the line between personal and professional life, leading to a constant "on" mentality that can quickly drain mental resources. Leaders face the challenge of supporting mental well-being without the traditional structure of the office environment, which means innovating new ways to promote mental clarity and focus from afar.

> Example: Companies like Atlassian and Dropbox offer remote-friendly mental wellness resources, from online mindfulness training to access to virtual counselors. Leaders who encourage remote workers to set boundaries and take breaks have found that these employees report higher engagement levels, fewer burnout symptoms, and greater job satisfaction.

Boosting Brain Health: Science-Backed Strategies for Success

1. Exercise for Cognitive Function

Physical health is closely tied to cognitive function. Regular physical activity increases blood flow to the brain, stimulating neuron growth and enhancing mental sharpness. Researchers at the University of British Columbia discovered that aerobic exercise can improve memory and learning by increasing hippocampal volume—the brain region crucial for these functions. For business professionals, this means that regular exercise can sharpen memory, aid in decision-making, and even increase creative problem-solving.

> Example: Leaders like Richard Branson attribute their high energy levels and mental clarity to their daily exercise routines. By integrating short bursts of physical activity throughout the day, leaders can boost their cognitive performance, enabling them to tackle complex challenges more effectively.

2. Nourishing the Brain: The Role of Nutrition

Like any high-performance machine, the brain needs proper fuel. Nutritional science shows that diets high in omega-3 fatty acids, antioxidants, and essential vitamins support cognitive function. Omega-3s, in particular, promote neuronal flexibility, allowing for faster information processing. The impact is clear: leaders who eat to nourish their brains can enhance memory, sustain energy, and sharpen problem-solving abilities.

> Statistic: Adults who consume omega-3-rich diets score up to 26% higher on cognitive function tests than those with lower omega-3 intake, according to a study published in "Neurology." This demonstrates the critical role nutrition plays in mental performance, providing leaders with a dietary tool to enhance their professional capabilities.

3. Sleep: The Hidden Productivity Booster

Quality sleep is crucial for mental performance. Sleep deprivation impairs creativity, reduces memory retention, and can lead to poor judgment. A "Nature" study showed that individuals who consistently sleep fewer than six hours perform at cognitive levels akin to intoxicated individuals—a clear disadvantage in high-stakes business environments.

> Statistic: The RAND Corporation estimates that sleep deprivation costs the U.S. economy up to $411 billion annually. Leaders who make sleep a priority benefit from enhanced cognitive function, more stable emotions, and improved decision-making, all of which are essential for sustained profitability.

Building a Brain-Healthy Culture for Lasting Success

1. Promoting a Mental Wellness Culture

Companies investing in mental health programs experience a significant return on investment. Deloitte found that mental health initiatives deliver a 4:1 return by reducing absenteeism, increasing productivity, and improving employee engagement. Leaders who foster a culture that values mental wellness create a workplace where resilience and productivity flourish.

> Example: Johnson & Johnson's mental health programs reduced depressive symptoms among employees by 33%, improving overall team morale and performance. By investing in employee well-being, organizations strengthen their workforce and create an environment that supports sustained success.

2. Encouraging Downtime for Mental Rejuvenation

The Pomodoro Technique, which alternates focused work with short breaks, is one effective way to maintain mental energy. Studies show that regular, brief breaks improve focus, creativity, and productivity. Leaders who advocate for structured breaks report higher-quality work, fewer errors, and greater job satisfaction among their teams.

> Statistic: Research from the Draugiem Group found that employees who took regular breaks were 11% more productive. Leaders who build downtime into their team's schedules see higher engagement levels and better work output, proving that a brain-friendly approach pays dividends.

Embracing the Brain-Wealth Connection

Understanding and leveraging the connection between mental wellness and business success is essential for future leaders. Embracing strategies that support brain health—such as exercise, proper nutrition, quality sleep, and structured downtime—gives business professionals an edge that's both tangible and measurable. As mental health continues to shape profitability, proactive investments in mental wellness will be the foundation for sustainable success. By prioritizing brain health, leaders not only empower themselves but create a pathway to profitability that's as resilient as it is rewarding.

Aspect	Statistic/Insight	Impact on Business
Mental Clarity & Decision-Making	Executives practicing mental clarity exercises report a **20-30% boost in decision-making speed and accuracy**.	Improved project outcomes, operational efficiency, and quicker product launches.
Focus & Productivity	High-performing individuals with deep focus generate **up to 5x more value** for their organizations.	Significant increase in productivity, driving revenue growth.
Stress & Productivity	Stress-related illnesses cost businesses around **$1 trillion globally** in lost productivity annually.	Companies prioritizing mental wellness see higher productivity and reduced absenteeism.
Remote Work & Mental Health	Companies supporting remote-friendly mental wellness resources report **higher employee engagement** and **reduced burnout**.	Enhanced employee satisfaction and job performance in hybrid and remote setups.
Exercise & Cognitive Function	Physical activity boosts memory and cognitive sharpness, with findings showing **increased hippocampal volume** linked to improved learning and memory.	Leaders with regular exercise routines report enhanced decision-making and creative problem-solving.
Nutrition & Cognitive Function	Adults with omega-3-rich diets perform **up to 26% better on cognitive function tests**.	Leaders eating brain-boosting diets experience better memory, energy, and problem-solving abilities.
Sleep & Productivity	Sleep deprivation costs the U.S. economy **up to $411 billion**	Quality sleep leads to better cognitive performance,

	annually; chronic sleep loss impairs cognitive function similarly to intoxication.	emotional stability, and decision-making, driving long-term profits.
Mental Health Programs ROI	Mental health initiatives yield a **4:1 return on investment** by reducing absenteeism and increasing productivity.	Enhanced team morale and performance, improving organizational resilience and success.
Structured Breaks	Employees taking regular breaks are **11% more productive** than those who work continuously without breaks.	Higher engagement, fewer errors, and increased productivity.

CHAPTER 3: STRESS RESILIENCE – TURNING ADVERSITY INTO ADVANTAGE

What would your life look like if every stressor became an opportunity for growth? How would your financial and personal success change if you mastered the art of turning pressure into performance? Can you envision a future where stress is not an enemy, but an ally in your pursuit of prosperity?

Stress is an unavoidable part of life, and in our fast-paced modern world, its presence has only intensified. The trick isn't to eliminate stress—an impossible feat—but to transform our response to it. This chapter dives deep into how building stress resilience not only protects mental and physical health but also amplifies financial success. To achieve this, we'll explore practical methods backed by science, compelling examples of resilience in action, and the undeniable link between handling stress effectively and thriving in your career and personal finances.

The Science of Stress Resilience

At its core, stress is a biological response that has evolved to protect us. When faced with perceived danger, the brain triggers a cascade of hormonal reactions, engaging the "fight-or-flight" mechanism. In moderation, this response is beneficial, sharpening focus and boosting energy. However, chronic stress—sustained over time—can wreak havoc on the body, leading to conditions such as hypertension, anxiety, and weakened immunity.

The concept of stress resilience refers to the ability to navigate and adapt to stress in a way that maintains or improves well-being. According to research from the American Psychological Association (APA), resilience isn't a trait that people either have or don't have; it involves behaviors, thoughts, and actions that anyone can learn and develop. By enhancing this skill, individuals are better equipped not just to withstand challenges but to thrive in their presence.

Real-World Examples of Turning Stress into Success

Consider the case of Sarah Blakely, the founder of Spanx. Before her product became a household name, Blakely faced a gauntlet of rejections from manufacturers and potential investors. Instead of allowing these rejections to erode her confidence, she adapted her approach. Blakely would pause, reevaluate her pitch, and refine her prototype, treating each setback as a learning opportunity rather than a failure. This mindset—pivoting under pressure—illustrates the essence of stress resilience. Her financial triumph with Spanx is now legendary, but it was the way she handled stress that positioned her for that breakthrough.

Another compelling example is Elon Musk. Known for his unyielding work ethic and ambitious ventures, Musk has encountered intense stress throughout his career—from nearly going bankrupt while funding Tesla and SpaceX to managing constant public scrutiny. Musk's approach to stress resilience involves problem-solving under pressure, a habit that has propelled his companies to the forefront of technology and space exploration. His success underscores a key principle: building the muscle of stress resilience turns potentially paralyzing moments into transformative ones.

The Health-Wealth Connection in Stress Management

So, why does stress resilience specifically impact financial success? The answer lies in the intersection of cognitive performance and emotional regulation. Stress can cloud judgment, impair decision-making, and stoke fear-based responses. A stressed-out mind is prone to impulsive actions—think rash spending, poor investment choices, or premature business decisions. Conversely, stress resilience supports clear thinking, strategic planning, and the confidence to make calculated risks that drive wealth accumulation.

For instance, a 2017 study published in The Journal of Occupational Health Psychology found that individuals who practiced mindfulness and stress management techniques reported higher job satisfaction and productivity. This uptick in productivity often leads to career advancement and higher earnings. Beyond the individual level, companies that prioritize stress resilience training for employees report better performance outcomes and higher retention rates. Google's mindfulness program, Search Inside Yourself, is a well-documented example, boosting both employee well-being and the company's innovative output.

Building Your Stress Resilience Toolkit

1. Mindfulness and Meditation: Regular meditation practices can alter the brain's response to stress. Research from Harvard Medical School shows that mindfulness reduces the density of the amygdala—the brain region associated with fear and anxiety—while strengthening connections in areas that regulate emotional response. This physiological shift allows for a more balanced, thoughtful reaction to stressors.

Try starting your day with just five minutes of guided meditation. Apps like Headspace or Calm offer sessions specifically designed for stress management. Over time, you'll notice that challenges that once triggered panic instead elicit a more measured, adaptive response.

2. Physical Exercise: Exercise isn't just good for your body; it's a powerful stress reliever. When you engage in physical activity, your body releases endorphins, which act as natural mood elevators. Moreover, regular exercise improves sleep quality and reduces overall

stress levels. For optimal benefits, aim for 30 minutes of moderate activity, such as brisk walking or cycling, at least five times a week.

3. Cognitive Reframing: This psychological technique involves changing your interpretation of a stressor. For example, instead of viewing a failed job interview as a definitive setback, see it as valuable feedback to refine your approach for the next opportunity. Cognitive reframing empowers you to see challenges as learning experiences, thereby reducing their emotional weight.

One corporate leader who mastered this is Jeff Bezos. Early in Amazon's journey, the company made costly mistakes, like investing in products that didn't sell as anticipated. Bezos, however, adopted a mindset that celebrated experimentation and iterative learning. Each stumble was a step toward future victories, cultivating a culture where stress was viewed as an inevitable and constructive part of innovation.

Practical Applications: The 4-Step Stress Audit

1. Identify: Write down the sources of your stress. Be specific—whether it's tight deadlines, financial pressures, or interpersonal conflicts.

2. Assess: Determine which stressors are within your control and which aren't. Redirect your energy toward those you can influence.

3. Adapt: Develop a plan for handling these stressors. This might mean setting clearer boundaries with work colleagues or automating parts of your financial management to reduce monthly worry.

4. Reflect: End each week by reviewing how you managed your stress. Note your successes and areas for improvement. Over time, this reflection builds self-awareness and a stronger resilience base.

Transforming Adversity into Growth

To truly leverage stress as a vehicle for financial success, it's crucial to shift your mindset from viewing stress as something harmful to recognizing its potential as a catalyst for growth. Embracing this shift doesn't mean denying the discomfort that stress can bring; rather, it means acknowledging that within that discomfort lies an opportunity.

During the 2008 financial crisis, many business owners faced seemingly insurmountable challenges. Yet, some adapted and thrived by pivoting their strategies. Take Howard Schultz of Starbucks, who, rather than focusing solely on cutbacks, doubled down on reinvigorating the customer experience and introducing new products. His approach allowed Starbucks not just to survive but to come out stronger, ultimately bolstering shareholder value and expanding the brand.

Final Thoughts: Building Wealth Through Resilience

The path to financial success is seldom linear. It's marked by unexpected detours, failures, and moments of intense pressure. Those who cultivate stress resilience position themselves to handle these challenges more effectively, making choices that safeguard both their well-being and their wallets. Think of stress resilience as a foundational skill—one that protects your health, fortifies your mindset, and amplifies your capacity to succeed financially.

Remember, the key isn't to wish away stress but to harness it. Every stressor carries the seeds of potential, waiting for you to turn it into your next advantage.

Cases, Statistics, and Models

What would your life look like if every stressor became an opportunity for growth? How would your financial and personal success change if you mastered the art of turning pressure into performance? Can you envision a future where stress is not an enemy, but an ally in your pursuit of prosperity?

Stress, in its multifaceted forms, can be both a stumbling block and a stepping stone. The essence of stress resilience lies in how one navigates these paths—whether stress leads to personal and professional breakthroughs or spirals into setbacks. Here, we will delve deeper into specific cases, statistical insights, and models for building stress resilience in both personal and professional contexts.

The Anatomy of Stress and Its Impacts: Key Statistics and Studies

To understand the importance of stress resilience, it's essential to recognize the scope of stress as a widespread issue. The American Institute of Stress highlights that approximately 33% of people report feeling extreme stress, while 77% experience stress that impacts their physical health, and 73% report that it affects their mental health. In the workplace, the cost of unaddressed stress is staggering, with stress-induced absenteeism and reduced productivity costing U.S. employers an estimated $300 billion annually. These figures underline that building stress resilience isn't just a personal benefit—it's an economic imperative.

A 2021 report by Gallup revealed that 57% of workers feel daily stress, particularly those in high-demand roles such as healthcare, finance, and education. These pressures often manifest as increased turnover rates, declining job satisfaction, and diminished organizational loyalty. On a global scale, the World Health Organization (WHO) has linked stress-related disorders to a 10% reduction in productivity, underscoring the direct correlation between mental health and economic performance.

Resilience in Action: Stories of Triumph

To illustrate the transformative power of stress resilience, real-world examples are invaluable. Consider the story of Indra Nooyi, former CEO of PepsiCo. Leading a global company, Nooyi faced relentless pressure. Rather than succumbing, she leaned on a network of advisors and mentors to reframe high-stakes challenges as opportunities for strategic pivoting. Her approach to stress resilience was methodical, involving reflection, delegation, and emotional intelligence. Under her leadership, PepsiCo's revenue grew from $35 billion in 2006 to $63.5 billion in 2017, illustrating that resilience can translate to outstanding financial outcomes.

Similarly, the case of Angela Duckworth, a psychologist and author known for her work on grit—a cousin to resilience—demonstrates the profound effects of persevering under pressure. Duckworth's research in academic settings showed that students who demonstrated high levels of grit outperformed their peers, even when those peers had higher IQs. The key takeaway: resilience amplifies results by maintaining focus and motivation during periods of challenge, bridging the gap between potential and achievement.

The Professional Model for Building Stress Resilience

In the professional sphere, building stress resilience involves structured strategies that can be implemented at individual and organizational levels. Below are models and best practices that illustrate this approach.

1. The Four A's of Stress Management Framework (Avoid, Alter, Adapt, Accept):

Developed as a practical guide, the Four A's framework helps professionals dissect stressors and respond effectively:

- Avoid: Whenever possible, steer clear of unnecessary stress. This could mean learning to say "no" to non-essential projects or delegating tasks that are outside one's primary competencies.

- Alter: Adjust situations to reduce the stress impact. For instance, clear communication and managing expectations with colleagues can mitigate misunderstandings and associated anxieties.

- Adapt: Change your approach to the stressor. This involves cognitive reframing, where challenges are viewed through a lens of potential learning and growth.

- Accept: Recognize what cannot be changed and work on emotional responses to these fixed stressors. Practices like gratitude journaling help to shift focus from stressors to positive aspects of life.

These elements combine to create a multi-layered response to stress, enabling professionals to maintain high performance without sacrificing their well-being.

2. The Resilience Wheel:

A tool developed by psychologists, the Resilience Wheel outlines six essential areas for building resilience:

- Self-Awareness: The ability to understand personal stress triggers and emotional responses.

- Mindfulness: Incorporating daily mindfulness exercises to maintain present-moment awareness.

- Self-Care: Prioritizing physical health through exercise, balanced nutrition, and sleep.

- Support Systems: Building a network of colleagues, mentors, or support groups.

- Purpose and Values: Aligning work and life goals with deeper values to provide motivation during tough times.

- Problem-Solving Skills: Strengthening the capacity to devise creative solutions under pressure.

Organizations like SAP have successfully implemented resilience training programs based on these principles, leading to reported improvements in team dynamics and productivity.

Personal Case Studies and Approaches to Resilience

Resilience isn't only vital for professional success; it's foundational for personal growth. The stories of ordinary individuals overcoming extraordinary challenges provide a rich context for understanding how resilience manifests in daily life.

Case Study: The Journey of J.K. Rowling:

Before her rise to fame as the author of the Harry Potter series, J.K. Rowling faced significant adversity, including poverty, single parenthood, and multiple rejections from publishers. Her story is an archetype of stress resilience: facing repeated discouragement, Rowling continued to revise her manuscript, motivated by her unwavering belief in her story's worth. This relentless pursuit, born of resilience, ultimately led to one of the most successful literary franchises in history.

The Data Behind Personal Resilience:

The National Institutes of Health (NIH) reports that people who actively engage in resilience-building activities, such as social connections, volunteering, or participating in hobbies, are 60% more likely to report high life satisfaction. Furthermore, studies show that resilience training can decrease the risk of depression by up to 30%, proving its profound effects on mental health.

Practical Recommendations for Personal Resilience:

1. Develop a Routine: Structure brings predictability, which reduces the mental load of decision-making during stressful periods. A morning routine that incorporates physical activity, time for reflection, or quiet time can serve as an anchor for the rest of the day.

2. Set Micro-Goals: Large challenges can feel insurmountable, but breaking them down into smaller, achievable goals helps maintain momentum and boosts morale with each milestone reached.

3. Learn to Detach and Recharge: Taking purposeful breaks isn't a sign of weakness—it's a strategy for resilience. Whether through a 15-minute walk, a lunch with a friend, or practicing deep-breathing exercises, brief respites help reset the mind.

Integrating Resilience into Personal Finances

Stress has a tangible impact on financial decisions. A study by the Journal of Behavioral Decision Making found that individuals under stress are more likely to make impulsive financial choices, which can lead to regrettable investments or excessive debt. Therefore, integrating resilience into one's financial habits is crucial for sustaining long-term economic health.

Budgeting with a Resilient Mindset:

1. Prepare for the Unexpected: Building an emergency fund of at least 3-6 months' worth of expenses acts as a financial buffer, reducing the stress associated with job loss or unforeseen expenses.

2. Automate Savings: Automating a percentage of income to go directly into a savings account prevents the emotional stress of manually allocating funds and builds financial security passively.

3. Mindful Spending: Applying mindfulness to financial transactions can curb unnecessary expenditures. Before making a purchase, pause and assess whether it aligns with long-term goals or is an emotional response to stress.

Case Study in Financial Resilience:

After the dot-com bubble burst in the early 2000s, thousands of tech workers lost their jobs and faced financial ruin. However, many who practiced financial resilience—those who lived below their means, invested prudently, and diversified their income sources—

weathered the downturn and emerged with greater financial stability. The key to their success was a proactive approach to stress resilience, applied to financial management.

Building Resilience: From Theory to Practice

Developing a Resilience Plan:

1. Set Clear Priorities: Identify the areas of your life and career that matter most. This clarity allows you to allocate energy efficiently and reduce stress tied to peripheral distractions.

2. Reflect Regularly: Keep a journal to note down stressful incidents and how they were handled. This not only builds self-awareness but also tracks progress in resilience-building.

3. Invest in Relationships: Whether professional or personal, having a network of supportive individuals can make a significant difference in managing stress. Regular check-ins with friends, family, or mentors help to maintain perspective and alleviate feelings of isolation.

Implementing Organizational Resilience Programs:

Companies should consider integrating resilience training as part of their employee development programs. Initiatives like stress management workshops, team-building retreats, and flexible working arrangements are not mere perks—they are investments that improve job satisfaction and retention.

Case Study: PwC's "Be Well, Work Well" Initiative:

Professional services firm PwC launched an initiative that focused on employee well-being and resilience through workshops, one-on-one coaching, and digital tools for mindfulness and stress management. The result was a marked increase in employee engagement and productivity. The program demonstrated that investing in resilience yields significant returns in terms of morale and business success.

The Resilience Dividend

Stress is inevitable, but how we respond to it shapes our path to success or stagnation. Stress resilience is the linchpin that converts challenges into catalysts for growth, safeguarding mental health while bolstering financial and professional achievements. By embedding resilience into both personal habits and professional practices, individuals and organizations alike can turn adversity into an undeniable advantage.

Aspect	Key Statistics	Case Studies/Examples	Practical Approaches
Prevalence of Stress	- 33% report extreme stress. - 77% physical impact. - 73% mental health impact.	General workforce statistics; WHO links stress to a 10% productivity drop.	Implement stress audits and resilience frameworks (e.g., 4 A's).
Economic Impact	- $300 billion annual cost due to productivity loss in U.S.	Company turnover and absenteeism costs; high-impact industries like healthcare and finance.	Introduce resilience training programs in companies.
Professional Resilience	- 57% of workers feel daily stress.	SAP's resilience programs boosting team dynamics and productivity.	Adopt models like the Resilience Wheel and cognitive reframing.
Personal Resilience	- 60% report higher satisfaction when engaging in resilience activities.	J.K. Rowling's rise despite poverty and rejections; Angela Duckworth's *grit* research.	Establish routines, set micro-goals, and build support networks.
Financial Decisions	- Poor financial choices linked to high stress (Journal of Behavioral Decision Making).	Financial resilience during the dot-com crash.	Build emergency funds, automate savings, and practice mindful spending.

Organizational Initiatives	- Programs improve job satisfaction and retention (e.g., PwC).	PwC's "Be Well, Work Well" initiative increased engagement.	Implement well-being programs and stress management workshops.

CHAPTER 4: HEALTHY HABITS, WEALTHY MINDSET – DAILY ROUTINES THAT BUILD BOTH HEALTH AND PROSPERITY

Have you ever wondered why some people seem to have it all—energy, well-being, and wealth—while others struggle endlessly just to stay afloat? It's not a secret; it's a formula hidden in plain sight, deeply woven into the habits we cultivate. In understanding this, we don't just bridge the gap between health and wealth; we fuse them into an inseparable force that fuels lasting success.

As Simon Sinek, the influential author and motivational speaker, famously stated: "Success is not a random act. It arises out of a predictable and powerful set of circumstances and behaviors." In essence, the routines we practice each day don't just shape our bodies; they mold our mindset, our opportunities, and our financial trajectory. From age-old proverbs to modern psychological studies, history affirms that habits are at the root of personal and professional achievement.

The Historic Power of Routine: A Timeless Secret

The concept of daily routines as a driver for success is far from new. In ancient Greece, philosophers like Aristotle mused on the power of repeated action. "We are what we repeatedly do. Excellence, then, is not an act, but a habit." Fast forward to the industrial age, when figures like Thomas Edison and Nikola Tesla, in their contrasting styles, demonstrated that the disciplined organization of time and habits paved the way for groundbreaking inventions and sustained productivity.

Edison was known for keeping erratic hours but was relentless in his pursuit, sticking to a personal set of practices that kept his mind and body tuned for discovery. Tesla, on the other hand, maintained strict patterns that aligned with his belief in preserving mental and physical health as part of his innovation strategy. These pioneers embodied the intertwined nature of rigorous habits and monumental output, a principle that stands today.

In modern terms, wellness science has illuminated what the ancients intuited: physical and mental health directly influence productivity and financial capability. Decades of research now show that integrating specific health-focused routines into daily life can catalyze financial growth. Yet, why does this connection exist, and what does it look like in practice?

Morning Routines: The Foundation for a Prosperous Day

The morning ritual has been a consistent hallmark of highly successful individuals throughout history and across fields. The first hour upon waking is when the brain is at its most receptive state, an ideal period for setting intentions and reinforcing mental clarity. This window, often termed the "golden hour," allows us to prime our minds for the challenges of the day while nurturing our bodies

Consider this: Richard Branson, the entrepreneur behind Virgin Group, credits much of his success to starting the day with physical activity. Whether it's a run, a swim, or a round of tennis, Branson believes that exercise clears the mind and creates energy that lasts throughout the day. "Exercise and play are key not only to physical health but to creative thinking," he has said in numerous interviews.

Scientific studies back this up, highlighting the role of exercise in releasing endorphins that enhance mood and cognitive function. This neurobiological boost is essential for decision-making, a cornerstone of financial success. The connection is clear: a robust morning routine fuels not only the body but also sharpens the mind's acuity for critical thought and strategic planning.

But a successful morning isn't only about physical activity. Meditation, gratitude journaling, and reading are other cornerstones found in the habits of top achievers. Meditation, for instance, trains the mind to remain calm under pressure—a skill directly transferable to high-stakes financial decisions. Gratitude journaling shifts focus to what one has, fostering a mindset of abundance that invites more of the same.

The Compounding Effects of Consistency

James Clear, author of Atomic Habits, emphasizes that the power of habits lies in their compounding effect. He states, "Habits are the compound interest of self-improvement. Getting 1% better every day counts for a lot in the long run." This principle applies to health and wealth alike. The repeated practice of wellness habits doesn't just maintain the status quo; it creates exponential growth over time.

Let's break down the science. Regular exercise, mindfulness practices, and balanced nutrition contribute to reduced cortisol levels, which in turn minimizes the long-term impacts of stress—a silent wealth drainer. High cortisol levels have been linked to impaired cognitive function, disrupted sleep, and emotional imbalance, all of which can hinder effective decision-making and productivity.

Think about the practice of simple daily reflection. Spending ten minutes each evening reviewing the day's events helps consolidate learning and insights. This habit creates a feedback loop that enhances problem-solving abilities and prepares the mind for future challenges. It's not just about reviewing victories but also failures, which transforms them into stepping stones for financial and personal growth. This introspective habit is found in the lives of luminaries like Warren Buffett, who has often spoken about the value of taking time to think without distraction.

Health as an Investment, Not an Expense

One perspective that bridges the gap between wellness and financial prosperity is viewing health not as a cost but as an investment. In the past, the narrative was different. The idea of dedicating time and resources to health was often seen as a luxury. Today, research and high-performance case studies tell us otherwise. It is now clear that neglecting health in the pursuit of financial goals is a short-sighted approach that can backfire over time.

The tech world provides a stark illustration of this evolving mindset. Take Jeff Bezos, founder of Amazon, who emphasizes getting eight hours of sleep as a non-negotiable. Bezos has been quoted saying, "I think better. I have more energy. My mood is better," attributing his decision-making prowess to proper rest. This habit directly counters the old image of the sleepless executive who sacrifices health at the altar of success. Modern CEOs, business leaders, and entrepreneurs increasingly understand that energy management—rooted in quality sleep, diet, and exercise—is the new time management.

So, what does this mean for the average person striving for financial stability? The shift toward viewing health as an asset requires rethinking priorities. Investing time in sleep, exercise, and nutrition isn't taking away from productivity; it's fueling it. Those who adopt this mindset find themselves more resilient, adaptive, and capable of meeting challenges head-on.

The Future: Technology and Integrated Habits

Looking ahead, the future of health-wealth synergy will likely see more integration with technology. Innovations in wearable tech, artificial intelligence, and personalized health tracking are already making it easier to maintain beneficial habits and monitor their impacts on performance. Imagine a world where your fitness tracker not only records your steps and heart rate but also advises on the most optimal time for strategic thinking based on your circadian rhythm and stress markers.

This future isn't far off. Already, apps exist that synchronize meditation reminders with productivity logs, reinforcing a balance between intense focus and mental rest. The merging of these tools will bring about an era where well-being and performance are not just managed but enhanced through real-time feedback.

A Call to Habit

As you step into this fusion of health and wealth, remember that building a prosperous mindset begins with small, intentional steps. Challenge yourself to start by anchoring one habit—perhaps a ten-minute morning meditation or a mid-day walk. As Sinek might say, start with "why." Why do these habits matter to you? What deeper purpose do they serve in your life?

By viewing health and wealth as two sides of the same coin, you unlock a powerful synergy that transcends traditional notions of success. You transform your routines from simple acts of discipline to meaningful rituals that propel you toward a healthier, wealthier future.

Why Do Companies Fail in Integrating Health and Wealth Practices?

Despite the mounting evidence that health-focused habits lead to financial gains, many organizations struggle to embed these practices into their corporate culture. But why? What stands in the way of a seamless connection between wellness and prosperity within the framework of modern business?

For many companies, the failure lies in a short-term mindset. Businesses often prioritize immediate profits and shareholder value over the well-being of their employees. The emphasis is on productivity at any cost, perpetuating a culture that sees wellness initiatives as "nice-to-have" perks rather than essential investments. This perspective is rooted in a traditional view where success is equated with long hours and tireless commitment, irrespective of the physical and mental toll.

However, evidence suggests this approach is flawed. According to a report from the American Psychological Association, work-related stress costs businesses billions in lost productivity, absenteeism, and health expenses each year. Yet, despite these statistics, wellness programs are frequently underfunded, poorly implemented, or seen as fringe benefits disconnected from core business operations.

Simon Sinek's insight, "Leadership is not about being in charge. It is about taking care of those in your charge," highlights the gap many organizations fail to bridge. Companies that prioritize employee well-being as part of their growth strategy find that these efforts pay dividends in the form of increased engagement, reduced turnover, and sustained productivity. Those that don't often pay the price of employee burnout, disillusionment, and a tarnished reputation.

Personal Struggles with Managing Health and Wealth

On an individual level, managing the intersection of health and financial success is equally challenging. The reasons are multifaceted, ranging from ingrained habits and cultural expectations to societal pressures. Why do so many of us struggle to balance the two?

1. Overworking as a Badge of Honor: In many cultures, particularly in fast-paced, high-achieving societies, long hours are often seen as a testament to dedication. The U.S., for instance, has cultivated a "hustle culture" where relentless work is glorified, and sleep is minimized in pursuit of ambition. Yet, the consequences are well-documented: increased

rates of anxiety, chronic illness, and diminished cognitive capacity. The cycle of pushing for financial success at the expense of health is self-defeating and unsustainable.

2. Lack of Time and Energy: A common refrain is, "I don't have time to exercise" or "I'm too tired to cook a healthy meal after work." When life's demands pile up, health routines are often the first to be sacrificed. However, this choice undermines the very productivity and energy required for financial pursuits. The paradox is that those who make time for wellness often find they have more time and focus to excel in their work.

3. Immediate vs. Long-term Gratification: Managing both health and wealth requires thinking long-term, a mindset that conflicts with human nature's preference for immediate rewards. Choosing an evening jog over binge-watching a show or preparing a balanced meal over ordering takeout involves delaying gratification. This mental shift can be difficult, particularly in a world where convenience is king.

Global Perspectives on Managing Health and Wealth

Different cultures offer varied approaches to balancing health and financial success, providing valuable lessons and insights into how these challenges can be met. By examining practices across the globe, we can identify what works, what doesn't, and why.

Japan: Discipline and Harmony

Japan is a standout when it comes to integrating health and professional life. Rooted in values of discipline, respect, and balance, the Japanese culture places significant emphasis on ikigai, the concept of a "reason for being." This approach emphasizes aligning daily work with a sense of purpose, fostering both mental well-being and sustainable productivity.

Yet, Japan is also known for its intense work culture. Karoshi, a term that translates to "death from overwork," is a sobering reminder of the dark side of extreme dedication. This paradox illustrates the challenge of balancing the value of hard work with the need for rest and rejuvenation. To counteract this, some Japanese companies have begun implementing policies such as mandatory vacation days and designated "no overtime" evenings to encourage work-life balance.

Europe: A Holistic View of Work-Life Balance

European countries, particularly those in Scandinavia, have long been recognized for their progressive attitudes toward work-life balance. In Denmark and Sweden, for example, the idea of fika (a coffee and cake break) represents more than just a pause; it is a cultural practice that encourages reflection, social connection, and mental recharge. These habits are not just socially accepted but embedded into the fabric of daily work life.

The European approach often includes shorter workweeks and generous vacation policies, which studies have shown correlate with higher productivity and greater well-being. The

European model challenges the myth that long hours equal better output. By valuing time off, employees return to work more energized and with a healthier mindset, which in turn supports more effective decision-making and creativity.

This model is not without its criticisms. Some argue that such a relaxed approach may not be as effective in highly competitive industries where rapid growth is essential. Yet, even in fast-paced sectors, there's growing acknowledgment that a sustainable, health-centric approach ultimately leads to stronger long-term financial outcomes.

Latin America: Social Bonds and Community

In Latin America, the concept of familismo, which prioritizes family and community, plays a central role in daily life. This cultural emphasis fosters strong social networks, providing emotional support that contributes to both mental health and financial stability. Latin American work environments often reflect these values, placing importance on personal connections and social interactions.

However, economic pressures and job market instability in some Latin American countries can force individuals into long hours and multiple jobs, compromising their health for financial survival. Addressing these challenges requires policies that recognize the importance of community well-being alongside individual health. Efforts like integrating wellness programs and encouraging flexible work arrangements could bridge the gap between financial necessity and health maintenance.

The U.S.: The Hustle Culture and Its Consequences

The U.S. has long been characterized by a relentless drive for success. The "American Dream" fuels ambition, fostering an environment where work often dominates life. This drive has led to remarkable innovation and wealth creation, but it comes at a cost. Burnout, stress-related illnesses, and a dependence on fast-paced, high-calorie diets are pervasive.

Yet, within this hustle culture, a counter-movement is growing. Companies like Google and Salesforce have pioneered initiatives to integrate wellness into their corporate cultures. Free fitness classes, nap pods, and mental health days are examples of efforts to support employee well-being. While these benefits are significant, they often cater primarily to the tech industry and large corporations, leaving smaller companies struggling to implement similar practices due to budget constraints.

India: Tradition Meets Modern Struggles

In India, traditional practices like yoga and Ayurveda have long highlighted the importance of balancing physical, mental, and financial health. Yoga, with its focus on mindfulness, flexibility, and breathwork, aligns closely with modern understandings of stress management and cognitive function. The practice is not only a health intervention but a way to center the mind, preparing individuals for clearer thinking and better decision-making.

Despite these deep-rooted practices, rapid urbanization and economic growth have introduced Western work habits, including extended hours and competitive work environments. The blending of traditional health practices with modern corporate life is a work in progress. Progressive Indian companies are beginning to bring these traditions into the workplace through wellness programs that integrate yoga and meditation as part of the daily routine.

Facing the Challenge: Learning Across Borders

So, how can we, as individuals and organizations, bridge the gap between health and wealth management? The answer may lie in synthesizing the strengths of each culture while recognizing and overcoming shared weaknesses.

1. Creating Sustainable Systems: Companies can borrow from Japan's discipline and Europe's work-life integration to create sustainable work environments. Policies that enforce regular breaks and respect for personal time can prevent the exhaustion that sabotages long-term productivity.

2. Education and Awareness: On an individual level, there needs to be greater awareness about the benefits of managing health as an investment. Employers and policymakers can offer workshops and training programs that equip individuals with the tools to create their own sustainable habits.

3. Leveraging Technology: As we look to the future, technology will play a pivotal role in helping manage the balance between health and productivity. Whether through apps that remind us to move during the day, AI tools that optimize our schedules for peak performance, or biometric devices that monitor stress levels, these tools can help integrate wellness into our daily routines in a personalized way.

4. Cultural Sensitivity and Customization: Any strategy for integrating health and wealth management must be culturally adaptive. What works in a Nordic country with high social trust may need tailoring for a competitive U.S. corporate environment or for a collectivist society like those in Latin America. The key is to respect cultural values while introducing new practices that enhance both health and financial well-being.

What if we shifted our collective mindset? What if we viewed health not as a diversion from work but as an essential driver of it? The global perspectives we've explored reveal that balancing health and financial success isn't just a personal battle; it's a cultural endeavor. While the challenges are nuanced and varied, the underlying truth remains: those who manage to align their health practices with their financial goals are not only more likely to achieve success but sustain it.

Whether through Japan's disciplined mornings, Europe's protected leisure, Latin America's community bonds, the U.S.'s evolving corporate wellness trends, or India's meditative practices, each offers lessons. By embracing this global tapestry of insights, we can cultivate a mindset where health and wealth are not competing interests but complementary partners on the path to sustained prosperity.

Culture/Region	Approach to Health and Wealth Management	Strengths	Challenges
Japan	Discipline and balance through the concept of *ikigai*. Implementation of mandatory vacation days and "no overtime" evenings.	Strong work ethic, focus on purpose and harmony.	Intense work culture, risk of *karoshi* (death from overwork).
Europe (Scandinavia, etc.)	Progressive work-life balance policies, shorter workweeks, emphasis on breaks like *fika*.	High productivity, well-rested employees, higher job satisfaction rates.	May be less effective in highly competitive industries requiring intensive work.
Latin America	Focus on *familismo*, strong social connections, prioritization of family and community.	Emotional support networks that enhance mental health and stability.	Economic pressures leading to long hours and multiple jobs, impacting health.
United States	"Hustle" culture, success associated with long working hours. Larger companies implement wellness initiatives.	Innovation and strong entrepreneurial drive, growing adoption of wellness programs.	High stress levels, reliance on fast food, wellness policies often limited to large corporations.
India	Integration of traditional practices like yoga and *Ayurveda* into daily life and	Strong heritage of health and mindfulness practices.	Rapid urbanization and adoption of Western work

	modern workplaces.		habits, introducing work-related stress.

CHAPTER 5: INVESTING IN YOURSELF – THE ROI OF HEALTH-CENTRIC LIFESTYLES

I magine for a moment that you're the CEO of a company, not just any company but the most significant enterprise you'll ever manage: yourself. As the head of this enterprise, you have two primary resources to allocate—your time and your energy. How you manage these resources directly affects the company's bottom line: your personal success, financial prosperity, and overall happiness.

In this chapter, we will explore how a commitment to health-centric living can yield not just qualitative improvements like greater life satisfaction but quantifiable financial returns as well. We'll delve into real-life examples, research-backed insights, and a roadmap for integrating these principles into your daily life to maximize your "return on investment" (ROI).

The Foundation of Personal Capital: Your Health

Before we examine the economic impact of health, let's establish why it is the cornerstone of personal capital. The World Health Organization (WHO) defines health as "a state of complete physical, mental, and social well-being." In the same way that a company's infrastructure and workforce are essential for productivity, your physical and mental health form the backbone of your ability to earn, create, and thrive.

Think about this: Have you ever tried to make critical financial decisions or manage a high-stakes meeting while feeling under the weather or severely stressed? It's likely that your decision-making skills were compromised, and your productivity dipped. Conversely, when you're well-rested, nourished, and in a positive mental state, your problem-solving abilities and creativity are at their peak. It's no coincidence that some of the most successful people in business, like Jeff Bezos and Warren Buffett, prioritize getting enough sleep and practicing mindfulness.

The Hidden Costs of Neglect

Investing in health-centric practices isn't just about reaping benefits; it's also about avoiding the hidden costs associated with poor health. The American Journal of Health Promotion reported that employees with poor health habits incurred up to 147% higher health care costs compared to their healthier peers. Now, extend this analogy to your financial life. The costs of untreated stress, poor nutrition, and inadequate physical activity manifest as reduced work performance, more sick days, and higher medical expenses—all of which impact your earnings.

Consider this scenario: John, a 35-year-old software developer, is driven by his career goals but neglects his health, frequently working late, eating fast food, and skipping exercise. Initially, his focus on work seems to yield results—he earns promotions and bonuses. However, after a few years, chronic fatigue and stress lead to a series of health issues. Medical bills, a week-long hospitalization, and a forced break from work lead to significant financial setbacks. On the other hand, Sarah, a colleague who values her well-being, practices daily meditation, hits the gym, and eats a balanced diet. Her energy levels and mental acuity allow her to sustain peak performance without burnout, translating to consistent earnings and fewer medical expenses.

Ask yourself: Which of these outcomes do you want for your own story?

The Economic Case for Health-Centric Living

1. Higher Productivity Equals Higher Income

The data speaks for itself. A study by the Harvard Business Review found that employees who engage in regular exercise are 15% more productive than their inactive peers. That productivity boost translates to higher earnings potential. For entrepreneurs, the benefits are even more pronounced; maintaining mental clarity and physical stamina can be the difference between seizing an opportunity and missing out.

Imagine that you're an investor evaluating two startups. One founder burns the midnight oil relentlessly, sacrificing sleep and exercise to push through. The other practices balanced work habits, takes time to recharge, and engages in regular exercise. Who would you bet on for long-term success? The founder who prioritizes health will likely outpace their overextended counterpart because they'll sustain energy and clarity to drive innovation.

2. Reduced Healthcare Costs: A Direct Financial Benefit

Preventive healthcare—through diet, exercise, and regular wellness checks—drastically reduces the likelihood of chronic conditions like diabetes, hypertension, and heart disease. According to the CDC, nearly 90% of the nation's $4.1 trillion in annual healthcare expenditures are for people with chronic and mental health conditions. By investing in a healthier lifestyle, you mitigate these risks and reduce your future medical expenses.

Consider another example: Lisa, a financial analyst, made a conscious decision at age 30 to adopt a plant-based diet, participate in community yoga classes, and limit her alcohol consumption. Over the next 15 years, she reported fewer sick days and spent significantly less on medical treatments compared to her colleagues. The savings she accumulated from these medical expenses were eventually funneled into investments that compounded over time. Not only did she preserve her health, but she also improved her financial portfolio.

3. Mental Health as a Financial Catalyst

The often overlooked aspect of health-centric living is mental wellness, which has profound effects on earning potential and financial acumen. The American Psychological Association has linked high levels of chronic stress to cognitive decline and poor decision-making. By investing in practices that improve mental health—such as mindfulness, social connections, and hobbies—you're enhancing your brain's capacity for complex thought and strategic planning.

Picture a scenario where an executive, Emma, faces daily pressures from managing a multimillion-dollar project. Instead of surrendering to stress, she incorporates a 20-minute meditation practice into her morning routine. Over time, Emma notices a marked improvement in her ability to focus during high-stress meetings, foresee potential pitfalls, and make better decisions. The compound effect? Her leadership skills translate into career promotions, salary raises, and stock options, underscoring how mental health investments yield tangible financial outcomes.

A Step-by-Step Roadmap to Building Your Health Portfolio

Let's turn theory into actionable strategy. Just as you'd diversify your financial investments, a health-centric lifestyle requires a multi-faceted approach. Here's a plan to start:

Step 1: Physical Activity – The Minimum Effective Dose

Aim for at least 150 minutes of moderate aerobic exercise weekly. If time is an issue, try "exercise snacking," where you break activity into smaller, manageable chunks throughout the day. Research shows that even 10-minute bursts can boost cardiovascular health and mental alertness.

Step 2: Nutrition – Eating for Energy and Longevity

Swap processed foods for whole, nutrient-dense options. A balanced diet rich in lean proteins, healthy fats, and complex carbohydrates fuels sustained energy levels. Don't underestimate hydration—water is crucial for cognitive function and physical performance.

Step 3: Sleep – The Ultimate Force Multiplier

Aim for 7–9 hours of quality sleep per night. Consistent rest supports memory consolidation, stress management, and immune function. Think of sleep as your body's nightly maintenance routine, enhancing your productivity and preventing costly health issues.

Step 4: Mindfulness and Stress Reduction

Begin a simple mindfulness practice. Start with just 5 minutes of deep breathing or guided meditation each day. Apps like Headspace or Calm make it easier than ever to incorporate this practice into your routine. Over time, you'll find that your mind becomes more resilient to stress, allowing you to respond to challenges more thoughtfully.

Step 5: Social and Emotional Well-being

Invest in relationships that uplift you. Engaging in meaningful connections reduces stress and boosts mental health, enhancing your ability to tackle challenges head-on. This could mean prioritizing family dinners, joining a local club, or participating in volunteer work.

The path to a health-centric lifestyle isn't without effort. It requires discipline, planning, and often a shift in how we allocate time and resources. But consider this: the ROI isn't limited to dollars and cents. You'll experience gains in energy, resilience, and a renewed sense of purpose. You'll save on healthcare, increase your earnings potential, and extend your productive years.

Take a moment now and consider your current lifestyle. Are you prioritizing short-term gains at the expense of your health, or are you making consistent deposits into your wellness portfolio? The choice you make today will compound over time, yielding dividends that can change the trajectory of your personal and financial life. Investing in yourself isn't just wise—it's essential.

Avoiding Common Pitfalls and Future Challenges

After understanding the myriad benefits of adopting a health-centric lifestyle and its impact on financial success, it's crucial to delve into the mistakes that often derail even the most well-meaning individuals and organizations. This chapter focuses on the key errors to avoid, the challenges that lie ahead, and a real-world example of a company that has successfully integrated wellness principles to drive growth and prosperity.

Part 1: Common Pitfalls to Avoid in Health-Centric Living

1. Neglecting Consistency in Health Practices

One of the most common mistakes individuals make when investing in health is inconsistency. A burst of enthusiasm often leads to initial changes in diet, exercise, or mindfulness routines, but these efforts fade without a structured approach. Like any investment, the benefits of health practices accumulate over time. A one-month commitment to healthy eating or a brief stint at the gym isn't enough to achieve lasting results. Health should be viewed as a long-term investment, with daily habits acting as incremental contributions that compound over time.

Consider this: A CEO, well aware of the benefits of a balanced lifestyle, might initiate a corporate wellness program that starts strong but gradually dwindles due to a lack of ongoing support and engagement. The failure here isn't in starting the initiative, but in failing to create a culture that sustains it.

How to Avoid This: Create realistic, long-term plans for integrating health practices. Commit to daily or weekly check-ins with yourself, akin to financial reviews, to assess your progress and make necessary adjustments. Establishing accountability partners or leveraging technology, such as fitness and health-tracking apps, can help reinforce consistency.

2. Underestimating Mental Health

Another major oversight is focusing exclusively on physical wellness while neglecting mental health. The mind and body are deeply interconnected, and ignoring mental well-being undermines even the most disciplined physical health routines. Chronic stress, for example, can derail diet plans, reduce the effectiveness of exercise, and contribute to a range of physical health issues, such as hypertension.

Example: Many ambitious professionals fall into the trap of relentless work hours and dismiss stress management as a luxury. While they might make time for the gym or a nutritious meal, they overlook practices like meditation or social activities, leading to eventual burnout that compromises both health and career.

How to Avoid This: Treat mental health with the same seriousness as physical health. Schedule regular mental health breaks, practice mindfulness, and maintain hobbies or activities that bring joy and relaxation. Remember that a clear, focused mind improves your decision-making and overall productivity, providing substantial long-term returns.

3. Ignoring the Role of Community and Support Systems

A common mistake in pursuing a health-centric lifestyle is trying to go it alone. Whether due to pride, individualism, or the mistaken belief that wellness is a solo endeavor, many fail to harness the power of social support. Research consistently shows that strong social connections contribute to longer life expectancy, reduced stress, and improved mental health.

Think of a scenario: An entrepreneur launches a small startup, dedicating most waking hours to its growth. He begins with healthy practices, like morning workouts and nutritious meals, but as stress mounts, those habits fall by the wayside. Without a community to encourage him or share accountability, he reverts to long, isolated hours and poor habits.

How to Avoid This: Actively seek out support systems—friends, family, or like-minded groups—that can keep you motivated and accountable. Joining fitness clubs, participating in wellness challenges at work, or simply maintaining regular social engagements can make a significant difference.

4. Failing to Customize Your Approach

A significant pitfall is copying what works for others without adapting it to your own needs. For example, just because intermittent fasting works for a friend doesn't mean it will work for you. Similarly, a specific type of exercise that boosts someone else's productivity might not align with your body or schedule. A one-size-fits-all approach often leads to frustration and quitting.

How to Avoid This: Personalize your health investments. Conduct self-assessments or work with professionals—trainers, nutritionists, mental health experts—to tailor a plan that suits your unique needs, preferences, and limitations. Flexibility and personalization increase adherence and maximize outcomes.

Part 2: Future Challenges in Sustaining Health-Centric Lifestyles

As more people recognize the connection between wellness and financial success, the landscape is evolving. However, new challenges are emerging that could disrupt progress. Here are some of the primary obstacles we may face:

1. Technological Overload and Digital Fatigue

The rapid rise of digital technologies has made wellness practices more accessible but also introduced the paradox of screen fatigue. From fitness apps and video workout sessions to meditation apps, the reliance on screens has become a double-edged sword. Overuse of technology can lead to digital burnout, contributing to poor sleep quality, anxiety, and impaired focus.

Anticipating the Challenge: Strike a balance by incorporating tech-free wellness activities. Engage in nature walks, outdoor sports, or face-to-face interactions that don't require a screen. Be mindful of when and how often you use wellness apps and carve out digital detox times to give your mind a break.

2. Economic and Social Inequalities

As health-centric living becomes more mainstream, a divide may widen between those who can afford comprehensive wellness plans and those who cannot. Access to fresh produce, gym memberships, wellness retreats, and preventive healthcare can be limited by socioeconomic factors, leading to health and financial disparities.

Potential Solutions: Advocate for and support policies that promote public access to wellness resources. Volunteer or contribute to community programs that provide health education and activities. On an individual level, seek creative ways to maintain wellness on a budget—home workouts, simple meditation practices, and cooking with affordable, nutritious ingredients.

3. Sustainability and Wellness

The push for sustainable living adds another layer of complexity to health-centric practices. For example, certain health foods or supplements may not be eco-friendly, or gym equipment might be sourced unethically. Balancing personal health with environmental responsibility is becoming an increasing concern.

Navigating This Challenge: Prioritize sustainable wellness practices. Opt for local, organic produce and support businesses with ethical practices. Participate in community-driven events that combine wellness and sustainability, such as park cleanups with exercise groups or eco-friendly wellness workshops.

Part 3: Case Study – The Success Story of Patagonia

To illustrate how health-centric principles can translate to sustained financial success, we can look at Patagonia, an outdoor apparel company known for its commitment to environmental sustainability and employee well-being.

1. Emphasis on Work-Life Balance

Patagonia has long been a pioneer in creating a workplace that values health and balance. The company's headquarters in Ventura, California, features an on-site childcare center, allowing parents to balance work and family responsibilities. Flexible work schedules let employees surf when the waves are good, promoting physical activity and stress relief.

2. Mental and Physical Health Initiatives

Patagonia's emphasis on an active lifestyle isn't limited to its products; it's woven into its corporate culture. Employees are encouraged to take breaks, exercise, and engage in outdoor activities. This practice not only boosts morale but has been linked to increased creativity and problem-solving capabilities—traits that fuel innovation.

3. Investing in Sustainability as Part of Wellness

Patagonia's wellness philosophy extends beyond its staff. By championing environmental sustainability, the company aligns its values with broader community wellness. Its "Worn Wear" program, which promotes repairing rather than discarding old clothing, not only appeals to environmentally conscious consumers but also supports a culture of mindful consumption.

Results of These Initiatives

Patagonia's approach has led to impressive business results. The company reports low turnover rates compared to industry averages, indicating that employees are healthier, more satisfied, and more engaged. Financially, Patagonia's dedication to holistic wellness has attracted loyal customers who resonate with the brand's values, driving growth and profitability.

Takeaway for Individuals and Businesses: Patagonia exemplifies how investing in health and well-being, both on an individual and organizational level, generates dividends beyond traditional profit metrics. By integrating wellness into company culture, Patagonia has shown that a healthier workforce is a more productive, innovative, and loyal one.

The pursuit of a health-centric lifestyle isn't without its pitfalls or challenges, but by being aware of these potential obstacles, you can navigate them more effectively. Avoid the common mistakes of inconsistency, neglecting mental health, going it alone, and failing to personalize your approach. Prepare for future challenges by balancing technology use, advocating for wellness equity, and incorporating sustainable practices.

As Patagonia's example shows, when individuals and organizations prioritize wellness, they're investing not just in immediate productivity but in long-term resilience, innovation, and success.

Category	Common Mistakes to Avoid	Future Challenges	Real Example: Patagonia
Consistency Errors	Lack of consistency in adopting health practices	-	Internal programs promoting regular physical activity
Neglecting Mental Health	Focusing only on physical health, ignoring mental well-being	-	Encourages outdoor activities to reduce stress
Insufficient Social Support	Trying to implement health habits without community or support	-	Workplace environment that promotes work-life balance
Inadequate Personalization	Copying others' methods without adapting them to personal needs	-	Flexible wellness policies for employees
Technology Overload	-	Overuse of wellness apps and technology dependence	Balanced use of technology to support well-being
Economic and Social Inequality	-	Unequal access to wellness resources	Focus on community and sustainable initiatives
Sustainability and Wellness	-	Balancing wellness practices with	Programs like "Worn Wear"

		environmental responsibility	supporting conscious consumption
Positive Outcomes	-	-	Low employee turnover, high engagement, and financial growth

APPENDICES

Appendix A: Actionable Wellness Strategies for Financial Growth

When we consider the classic image of success, financial prosperity often comes to mind. However, this pursuit becomes deeply intertwined with a key, often overlooked component: health. Maintaining peak mental and physical well-being isn't just beneficial for life quality; it directly impacts financial performance. By incorporating these actionable wellness strategies, you can align your health practices to bolster your path toward financial growth.

1. Prioritize Quality Sleep

One of the most powerful yet underestimated wellness tools is sleep. Research consistently shows that adequate sleep enhances cognitive function, decision-making skills, and emotional regulation—all essential traits for effective money management. Studies from institutions like Harvard Medical School demonstrate that poor sleep not only impairs judgment but also increases impulsivity, making individuals prone to risky financial decisions.

Actionable Steps:

- Set a bedtime routine: Establish consistent sleeping and waking hours, even on weekends. This consistency reinforces your body's circadian rhythm.

- Create a sleep-friendly environment: Darken your room, reduce noise, and maintain a cool temperature.

- Limit screen time: Turn off electronic devices at least one hour before bedtime. The blue light from screens interferes with the production of melatonin, the sleep hormone.

2. Integrate Physical Activity into Your Routine

Exercise is more than a tool for staying fit; it is a catalyst for mental clarity and productivity. Regular physical activity increases the production of endorphins and helps manage cortisol levels, the stress hormone that can cloud judgment and lead to poor financial choices. Additionally, engaging in consistent physical activity has been linked to increased energy levels, which, in turn, boost work performance and income potential.

Actionable Steps:

- Start small: Incorporate at least 30 minutes of moderate activity like walking, jogging, or cycling into your daily schedule.

- Try desk exercises: If you have a sedentary job, integrate small, simple exercises such as leg stretches or seated twists to break up long periods of inactivity.

- Commit to a weekly plan: Schedule time for a mix of cardiovascular, strength training, and flexibility exercises.

3. Adopt Mindful Practices

Mindfulness and meditation have surged in popularity for good reason: they are key drivers of mental focus and stress reduction. Practicing mindfulness can reduce anxiety and enhance your ability to make thoughtful financial decisions. By becoming more present and aware, individuals learn to manage emotions that lead to impulse buying and poor financial habits.

Actionable Steps:

- Daily meditation: Dedicate 10-15 minutes each day to a guided meditation session using an app like Calm or Headspace.

- Mindful spending: Before making a purchase, pause to assess whether it aligns with your financial goals.

- Gratitude journaling: Keep a journal to write down things you're grateful for each day. This practice fosters contentment, which can reduce the tendency to seek fulfillment through unnecessary purchases.

4. Optimize Nutrition for Cognitive Excellence

What you eat fuels not only your body but also your brain. The connection between diet and mental performance is substantial, influencing everything from memory retention to problem-solving abilities. Eating a balanced diet filled with nutrient-dense foods promotes sustained energy, essential for productive workdays and the strategic thinking needed for financial growth.

Actionable Steps:

- Follow a brain-boosting diet: Incorporate omega-3 rich foods such as salmon, walnuts, and flaxseeds to support brain health.

- Hydrate consistently: Dehydration, even at mild levels, can impair cognitive functions. Aim for at least 8 glasses of water per day.

- Limit processed sugars: High sugar intake has been linked to mood swings and decreased cognitive function. Replace sugary snacks with healthier alternatives like fruit or nuts.

5. Foster Social Connections

Your network can have a profound impact on both your well-being and financial trajectory. Engaging with a supportive social circle reduces stress and contributes to emotional health. Strong relationships can open doors to financial opportunities, partnerships, and advice that can drive your financial success forward.

Actionable Steps:

- Nurture relationships: Spend quality time with friends and family. Emotional support not only enhances life satisfaction but can buffer against the stress that impacts financial decisions.

- Join professional groups: Participate in industry associations or community groups that align with your career or financial interests.

- Seek mentorship: Engage with mentors who inspire you and can offer guidance in balancing health and wealth.

Appendix B: Case Studies – Real Stories of Health-Driven Financial Success

Stories of real-life transformations provide powerful insights into how integrating wellness practices can lead to significant financial breakthroughs. Below are three case studies highlighting individuals who leveraged their health to achieve extraordinary financial outcomes.

Case Study 1: From Burnout to Business Boom – The Story of Rachel H.

Rachel H. was a driven marketing executive, often putting in 60-70 hour work weeks in pursuit of career advancement. However, the relentless pace led to chronic fatigue, frequent illness, and a decline in work quality. Realizing that her physical and mental health were deteriorating, Rachel committed to a wellness transformation.

Wellness Strategies Implemented:

- Routine Sleep Hygiene: Rachel began adhering to a strict sleep schedule, ensuring she got at least seven hours of rest each night.

- Regular Exercise Regimen: She started daily morning yoga sessions to energize her day.

- Balanced Diet: Rachel introduced a mix of lean proteins, complex carbohydrates, and healthy fats into her diet.

Outcome: Within months, Rachel noticed substantial improvements in her energy levels and focus. Her productivity at work surged, leading to a promotion. Inspired by her success, she started her own consulting business. Today, Rachel credits her decision to prioritize her well-being as the turning point that amplified her career and financial wealth.

Case Study 2: The Entrepreneur's Edge – How Mental Clarity Transformed Jack M.'s Start-up

Jack M., a tech entrepreneur, was ambitious and brimming with ideas, but he often struggled to prioritize and stay calm under pressure. His business faced delays due to his disorganized approach, and financial backers were beginning to express concerns. On the advice of a mentor, Jack turned to mindfulness and wellness coaching.

Wellness Strategies Implemented:

- Mindfulness Training: Jack committed to twice-daily meditation sessions that helped him improve focus and stress management.

- Nutritional Overhaul: He replaced fast food and caffeine binges with whole foods and nutrient-rich meals.

- Regular Breaks for Movement: Jack integrated short walking breaks into his workday.

Outcome: These changes allowed Jack to think more clearly and make strategic decisions with greater confidence. As a result, his company saw a turnaround, securing crucial investment funding. His newfound sense of balance not only fortified his mental health but also boosted his business's profitability, growing it into a multimillion-dollar enterprise.

Case Study 3: Balanced Living Leads to Investment Gains – Emily S.'s Story

Emily S., a financial analyst, believed that relentless dedication was the key to success. She skipped lunches and worked late, often sacrificing her health for the sake of her job. However, her growing anxiety and persistent fatigue started affecting her analytical abilities, resulting in poor investment choices. Emily decided it was time to pivot.

Wellness Strategies Implemented:

- Exercise and Nature Walks: Emily started jogging in a nearby park, which helped clear her mind and improve her mood.

- Scheduled Downtime: She blocked out time for herself each evening, engaging in activities she enjoyed, like reading and painting.

- Consistent Hydration: Emily focused on staying hydrated throughout her workday, which significantly reduced her headaches and improved her concentration.

Outcome: Emily's well-being initiatives rejuvenated her mental sharpness. Her improved focus and strategic thinking led to better portfolio management and investment picks, resulting in increased earnings and accolades from her firm. Over time, these changes not only improved her financial standing but also her satisfaction and fulfillment at work.

Aspect	Past	Present	Future	Figures	Recommendations
Awareness of Health's Role in Financial Success	Historically, health and wealth were often viewed as separate domains, with financial success prioritized over well-being. The impact of health on productivity and decision-making was poorly understood.	Growing recognition of the interplay between health and financial well-being, supported by modern studies. Wellness is seen as essential for career growth and entrepreneurial success.	Anticipated integration of health metrics into financial planning tools and corporate policies. Businesses may increasingly support wellness programs as strategic investments for financial outcomes.	Studies show that regular exercise can boost productivity by up to 21%, and adequate sleep can improve decision-making skills by 20-30%.	Prioritize health education as a foundational element in professional training programs. Integrate health analytics into financial planning.
Approach to Work and Productivity	The mindset favored long, grueling work hours with minimal breaks, often at the	Shift towards work-life balance, emphasizing efficiency and mental well-being. Flexible working	Automation and AI will allow more time for personal health management. Work environme	Gallup data shows that burned-out employees are 63% more likely to take a sick day.	Encourage structured breaks, mental health support, and a results-driven (not hours-driven) work culture. Implement

	expense of health. High burnout rates were common.	arrangements and wellness initiatives are on the rise.	nts will likely evolve to encourage physical activity and mindfulness.		policies that reduce stress and support well-being.
Nutrition and Cognitive Performance	Limited understanding of the link between nutrition and financial decision-making. Diets were often convenience-based, impacting energy and productivity.	Increased focus on nutritional habits as a contributor to mental acuity and sustainable energy. People are more aware of how diet influences focus and work output.	Predicted advances in personalized nutrition plans that optimize brain function and productivity. Corporate meal programs may incorporate brain-boosting foods.	Individuals who follow healthy eating patterns have a 25% increase in work performance, according to the World Health Organization (WHO).	Promote educational initiatives on nutrition's impact on cognitive function. Implement incentives for healthy eating in the workplace.
Stress Management	Stress was a sign of ambition; the culture around stress	Mindfulness, meditation, and mental health support are increasingly	Future trends include the use of VR and AI for immersive	A 2018 study reported that stress-related mental	Develop comprehensive mental health strategies, including daily mindfulness

	managemen t was sparse. Mental health concerns were often stigmatized.	seen as essential for maintaining professional effectiveness. Corporations adopt these as standard practices.	stress manageme nt experiences and personalize d mental health apps tailored for high-stress careers.	health issues contribute to annual productivit y losses exceeding $500 billion in the U.S.	practices, stress-relief breaks, and mental health workshops.
Workplace Design	Workspaces were designed for maximum productivity with little thought to employee well-being.	Ergonomic and health-focused designs are now incorporated into many modern workplaces. Standing desks, greenery, and open spaces are more common.	Future offices may feature biophilic design principles, active workstations, and communal wellness areas to encourage movement and social connection.	Research indicates that employees in well-designed spaces have a 15% higher well-being score, translating to better financial output.	Invest in office spaces that prioritize employee health. Include ergonomic equipment, encourage walking meetings, and create communal relaxation spaces.
Social Connections and Networking	Networking was transactional, with less emphasis on health	Recognized as a fundamental element of wellness, contributing	Future networking might emphasize community-building	A 2020 study showed that having strong social	Foster professional environments that emphasize supportive teamwork and

	impacts. Business relationships focused solely on financial gain.	to emotional support and strategic opportunities. The idea of holistic professional relationships is prevalent.	with a focus on shared well-being goals and cooperative growth models.	connections can increase life expectancy by 50% and boost productivity and job satisfaction.	mentoring relationships. Encourage collaborative events that focus on well-being and shared success.

END